W9-CQP-320

NINETEEN WAYS OF LOOKING
AT WANG WEI

NINETEEN WAYS OF LOOKING AT WANG WEI

How a Chinese poem is translated

Exhibit & Commentary by Eliot Weinberger
Further Comments by Octavio Paz

MOYER BELL LIMITED
Mt. Kisco, New York

Copyright © 1987 Eliot Weinberger and Octavio Paz
All rights reserved. First Edition 1987
Printed in the United States of America

For permission to reprint copyrighted material, the authors are indebted to the following:

Georges Borchardt Inc.: for the François Cheng translation, Copyright 1977 by Editions du Seuil.
Columbia University Press: for the Burton Watson translation, Copyright 1972 by the Columbia University Press; and for the H.C. Chang translation, Copyright 1977 by H.C. Chang.
Farrar Straus & Giroux: for the Witter Bynner & Kiang Kang Hu translation, Copyright 1978 by the Witter Bynner Foundation.
Indiana University Press: for the Donald A. Riggs & Jerome P. Seaton translation of François Cheng, Copyright 1982 by the Indiana University Press.
New Directions: for the Kenneth Rexroth translation, Copyright 1970 by Kenneth Rexroth.
Octavio Paz: for his translations, Copyright 1974, 1978 by Octavio Paz.
Penguin Books: for the G.W. Robinson translation, Copyright 1973 by G.W. Robinson.
Gary Snyder: for his translation, Copyright 1978 by Gary Snyder.
Charles E. Tuttle Co.: for the C.J. Chen & Michael Bullock translation, Copyright 1960 by Jerome Chen & Michael Bullock; and for the William McNaughton translation, Copyright in Japan 1974 by Charles Tuttle.
University of California Press: for the Peter A. Boodberg translation, Copyright 1979 by The Regents of the University of California.
University of Chicago Press: for the James J.Y. Liu translation, Copyright 1962 by James J.Y. Liu.
Wai-lim Yip: for his translation, Copyright 1972 by Wai-lim Yip.

An earlier version of Weinberger's essay first appeared in ZERO: CONTEMPORARY BUDDHIST THOUGHT, edited by Eric Lerner. Paz's original essay, plus a Spanish translation of Weinberger's essay by Ulalume González de León, first appeared in VUELTA (Mexico City). The translation of Paz's essay is by Eliot Weinberger.

Library of Congress Cataloging-in-Publication Data

Weinberger, Eliot.
    Nineteen ways of looking at Wang Wei.

    1. Wang, Wei, 701–761. Lu ch'ai. 2. Wang, Wei,
701–761—Translations. I. Wang, Wei, 701–761.
Lu ch'ai. Polyglot. 1985. II. Paz, Octavio, 1914–
III. Title.
PL2676.A683W4   1987   895.1'13   87-21654

ISBN 0-918825-14-8 (pbk.)

Poetry is that which is worth translating.

For example, this four-line poem, 1200 years old: a mountain, a forest, the setting sun illuminating a patch of moss. It is a scrap of literary Chinese, no longer spoken as its writer spoke it. It is a thing, forever itself, inseparable from its language.

And yet something about it has caused it to lead a nomadic life: insinuating itself in the minds of readers, demanding understanding (but on the reader's own terms), provoking thought, sometimes compelling writing in other languages. Great poetry lives in a state of perpetual transformation, perpetual translation: the poem dies when it has no place to go.

The transformations that take shape in print, that take the formal name of "translation," become their own beings, set out on their own wanderings. Some live long, and some don't. What kind of creatures are they? What happens when a poem, once Chinese and still Chinese, becomes a piece of English, Spanish, French poetry?

Here are 19 incarnations of a small poem by Wang Wei (c. 700–761), who was known in his lifetime as a wealthy Buddhist painter and calligrapher, and to later generations as a master poet in an age of masters, the Tang Dynasty. The quatrain is from a series of twenty poems on various sights near the Wang River (no relation). The poems were written as par of a massive horizontal landscape scroll, a genre invented by Wang. The painting was copied (translated) for centuries. The original is lost, and the earliest surviving copy comes from the 17th century: Wang's landscape after 1000 years of transformation.

1

(text)

鹿柴

空山不見人，
但聞人語響；
返景入深林，
復照青苔上。

The poem is by Wang Wei (c. 700–761), known in his lifetime as a wealthy Buddhist painter and calligrapher, and to later generations as a master poet in an age of masters, the Tang Dynasty. The quatrain is from a series of twenty poems on various sights near the Wang (no relation) River. The poems were written as part of a massive horizontal landscape scroll, a genre he invented. The painting was copied (translated) for centuries. The original is lost, and the earliest surviving copy comes from the 17th century: Wang's landscape after 900 years of transformation.

In classical Chinese, each character (ideogram) represents a word of a single syllable. Few of the characters are, as is commonly thought, entirely representational. But some of the basic vocabulary is indeed pictographic, and with those few hundred characters one can play the game of pretending to read Chinese.

Reading the poem left to right, top to bottom, the second character in line 1 is apparently a *mountain*; the last character in the same line a *person*—both are stylizations that evolved from more literal representations. Character 4 in line 1 was a favorite of Ezra Pound's: what he interpreted as an eye on legs; that is, the eye in motion, *to see*. Character 5 in line 3 is two trees, *forest*. Spatial relationships are concretely portrayed in character 3 of line 3, *to enter*, and character 5 of line 4, *above* or *on (top of)*.

More typical of Chinese is character 2 of line 4, *to shine*, which contains an image of the sun in the upper left and of fire at the bottom, as well as a purely phonetic element—key to the word's pronunciation—in the upper right. Most of the other characters have no pictorial content useful for decipherment.

2

(transliteration)

LÙ ZHĂI

Kōng shān bù jiàn rén

Dàn wén rén yǔ xiǎng

Fǎn jǐng (yǐng) rù shēn lín

Fù zhào qīng tái shàng

The transliteration is from modern Chinese, using the current, quirky *pinyin* system. Obvious, perhaps, to the Rumanians who helped develop it, but not to English speakers, is that the *zh* is a *j* sound, the *x* a heavily aspirated *s*, and the *q* a hard *ch*. The *a* is the *ah* of *father*.

Though the characters have remained the same, their pronunciation has changed considerably since the Tang Dynasty. In the 1920's the philologist Bernhard Karlgren attempted to recreate Tang speech; a transliteration of this poem, using Karlgren's system may be found in Hugh M. Stimson's *55 Tang Poems* (Yale, 1976). Unfortunately, the transliteration is written in its own forbidding language, with upside-down letters, letters floating above the words, and a leveled forest of diacritical marks.

Chinese has the least number of sounds of any major language. In modern Chinese a monosyllable is pronounced in one of four tones, but any given sound in any given tone has scores of possible meanings. Thus a Chinese monosyllabic word (and often the written character) is comprehensible only in the context of the phrase: a linguistic basis, perhaps, for Chinese philosophy, which was always based on relation rather than substance.

For poetry, this means that rhyme is inevitable, and Western "meter" impossible. Chinese prosody is largely concerned with the number of characters per line and the arrangement of tones—both of which are untranslatable. But translators tend to rush in where wise men never tread, and often may be seen attempting to nurture Chinese rhyme patterns in the hostile environment of a Western language.

3

(character-by-character translation)

Empty	mountain(s) hill(s)	(negative)	to see	person people
But	to hear	person people	words conversation	sound to echo
To return	bright(ness) shadow(s)*	to enter	deep	forest
To return Again	to shine to reflect	green blue black	moss lichen	above on (top of) top

* According to François Cheng, *returning shadows* is a trope meaning *rays of sunset*.

I have presented only those definitions that are possible for this text. There are others.

A single character may be noun, verb, and adjective. It may even have contradictory readings: character 2 of line 3 is either *jing* (brightness) or *ying* (shadow). Again, context is all. Of particular difficulty to the Western translator is the absence of tense in Chinese verbs: in the poem, what is happening has happened and will happen. Similarly, nouns have no number: rose is a rose is all roses.

Contrary to the evidence of most translations, the first-person singular rarely appears in Chinese poetry. By eliminating the controlling individual mind of the poet, the experience becomes both universal and immediate to the reader.

The title of the poem, *Lu zhai*, is a place-name, something like *Deer Grove*, which I take from a map of Illinois. It probably alludes to the Deer Park in Sarnath, where the Gautama Buddha preached his first sermon.

The first two lines are fairly straightforward. The second couplet has, as we shall see, quite a few possible readings, all of them equally "correct."

4

The Form of the Deer

So lone seem the hills; there is no one in sight there.

But whence is the echo of voices I hear?

The rays of the sunset pierce slanting the forest,

And in their reflection green mosses appear.

—W.J.B. Fletcher, 1919

The translation is typical of those written before the general recognition of Ezra Pound's *Cathay*, first published in 1915. Pound's small book, containing some of the most beautiful poems in the English language, was based on a notebook of literal Chinese translations prepared by the orientalist Ernest Fenollosa and a Japanese informant. The "accuracy" of Pound's versions remains a sore point: pedants still snort at the errors, but Wai-lim Yip has demonstrated that Pound, who at the time knew no Chinese, *intuitively* corrected mistakes in the Fenollosa manuscript. Regardless of its scholarly worth, *Cathay* marked, in T.S. Eliot's words, "the invention of Chinese poetry in our time." Rather than stuffing the original into the corset of traditional verse forms, as Fletcher and many others had done, Pound created a new poetry in English drawn from what was unique to the Chinese.

"Every force," said Mother Ann Lee of the Shakers, "evolves a form." Pound's genius was the discovery of the living matter, the force, of the Chinese poem—what he called the "news that stays news" through the centuries. This living matter functions somewhat like DNA, spinning out individual translations which are relatives, not clones, of the original. The relationship between original and translation is parent-child. And there are, inescapably, some translations that are overly attached to their originals, and others that are constantly rebelling.

Fletcher, like all early (and many later) translators, feels he must explain and "improve" the original poem. Where Wang's sunlight *enters* the forest, Fletcher's rays *pierce slanting*; where Wang states simply that voices are heard, Fletcher invents a first-person narrator who asks where the sounds are coming from. (And if the hills are *there*, where is the narrator?)

In line 4, ambiguity has been translated into confusion: Fletcher's line has no meaning. (What reflection where?) Or perhaps the line has a lovely and unlikely Platonic subtlety: if *their* refers to the mosses, then what *appears* is the reflection of moss itself.

Fletcher explains his curious (and equally Platonic) title with a note that *zhai* means "the place where the deer sleeps, its 'form'."

5
Deer-Park Hermitage

There seems to be no one on the empty mountain...

And yet I think I hear a voice,

Where sunlight, entering a grove,

Shines back to me from the green moss.

—Witter Bynner & Kiang Kang-hu, 1929

Witter Bynner was a primary purveyor of Chinoiserie translation in English in the 1920's—though not as extreme an exoticist as his Imagist counterparts, Amy Lowell and Florence Ayscough. His Chinese poet does however write from the ethereal mists of tentative half-perception: *there seems to be, and yet I think I hear.* (Wang, however, quite plainly sees no one and hears someone.)

Where Wang is specific, Bynner's Wang seems to be watching the world through a haze of opium reflected in a hundred thimbles of wine. It is a world where no statement can be made without a pregnant, sensitive, world-weary ellipsis. The *I* even hears a voice where the sunlight shines back to him from the moss. Such lack of sense was traditionally explained by reference to the mystical, inscrutable Fu Manchu East.

6

The Deer Park

An empty hill, and no one in sight

But I hear the echo of voices.

The slanting sun at evening penetrates the deep woods

And shines reflected on the blue lichens.

—Soame Jenyns, 1944

Dull, but fairly direct, Jenyns' only additions are the inevitable *I* and the explanatory *slanting* sun *at evening*. He is the only translator to prefer lichen to moss, though in plural form the word is particularly ugly.

In the fourth line *zhao* becomes both *shines reflected*, rather than one or the other, but he is still in the "reflected" trap: from what is the sun reflected?

Chinese poetry was based on the precise observation of the physical world. Jenyns and other translators come from a tradition where the notion of verifying a poetic image would be silly, where the word "poetic" itself is synonymous with "dreamy."

He might have squeaked by had he written *And shines reflected by the blue lichens*—accurate to nature, if not to Wang. But Jenyns—at the time Assistant Keeper of the Department of Oriental Antiquities at the British Museum, scribbling through the Blitz—was so far removed from the poem's experience that he found it necessary to add the following footnote to line 2: "The woods are so thick that woodcutters and herdsmen are hidden."

7

La Forêt

Dans la montagne tout est solitaire,

On entend de bien loin l'écho des voix humaines,

Le soleil qui pénètre au fond de la forêt

Reflète son éclat sur la mousse vert.

—G. Margouliès, 1948

[*The forest.* On the mountain everything is solitary, / One hears from far off the echo of human voices, / The sun that penetrates to the depths of the forest / Reflects its ray on the green moss.]

Margouliès prefers to generalize Wang's specifics: *Deer Grove* becomes, simply, *The Forest; nobody in sight* becomes the ponderous malaise of *everything is solitary.* In the second line he poeticizes the voices by having them come from *far off.* The French indefinite pronoun happily excludes the need for a narrator.

8

Deer Forest Hermitage

Through the deep wood, the slanting sunlight

Casts motley patterns on the jade-green mosses.

No glimpse of man in this lonely mountain,

Yet faint voices drift on the air.

—Chang Yin-nan & Lewis C. Walmsley, 1958

Chang and Walmsley published the first book-length translation of Wang Wei in English, but unfortunately their work bore little resemblance to the original.

In this poem, the couplets are reversed for no reason. The voices are *faint* and *drift on the air*. The mountain is *lonely* (surely a Western conceit, that empty = lonely!) but it's a decorator's delight: the moss is as green as jade and the sunlight *casts motley patterns*.

It is a classic example of the translator attempting to "improve" the original. Such cases are not uncommon, and are the product of a translator's unspoken contempt for the foreign poet. It never occurs to Chang and Walmsley that Wang could have written the equivalent of *casts motley patterns on the jade-green mosses* had he wanted to. He didn't.

In its way a spiritual exercise, translation is dependent on the dissolution of the translator's ego: an absolute humility toward the text. A bad translation is the insistent voice of the translator—that is, when one sees no poet and hears only the translator speaking.

9

The Deer Enclosure

On the lonely mountain

I meet no one,

I hear only the echo

of human voices.

At an angle the sun's rays

enter the depths of the wood,

And shine

upon the green moss.

—C.J. Chen & Michael Bullock, 1960

Chen and Bullock make some familiar "improvements": the first-person narrator, the *lonely* mountain, the sun *at an angle*. Wang's *see* becomes *meet* in their second line. Their main innovation is the creation of eight lines for Wang's four—a gesture that apparently caught them short when they had to break the last line into two.

10

On the empty mountains no one can be seen,

But human voices are heard to resound.

The reflected sunlight pierces the deep forest

And falls again upon the mossy ground.

—James J.Y. Liu, 1962

Liu's book, *The Art of Chinese Poetry*, applied the techniques of 1940's New Criticism to the interpretation of Chinese poetry. The New Critics preached strict attention to sense (special emphasis on learned irony) and the general neglect of music. Thus Liu's version is more accurate than most, but the first two lines heave, the third gasps, and the fourth falls with a thud on the mossy ground.

In the first line, by changing the expected *is* to *can be*, Liu has transformed Wang's specifics into a general and not terribly bright remark. *Human voices*, a steal from Eliot, is redundant; and the 19th century *resound* is only there to rhyme with *ground*. A ray of sunlight might *pierce* the deep forest, but *reflected sunlight* wouldn't, and absent from Liu's third line is the sense that it is late afternoon, that the sunlight is returning to the forest. In the fourth line, *green* has been subtracted, *ground* added.

In Liu's favor, however, are the absence of the "I" and the usual explanations.

Deep in the Mountain Wilderness

Deep in the mountain wilderness

Where nobody ever comes

Only once in a great while

Something like the sound of a far off voice.

The low rays of the sun

Slip through the dark forest,

And gleam again on the shadowy moss.

—Kenneth Rexroth, 1970

The taxonomy of Chinese translators is fairly simple. There are the scholars: most are incapable of writing poetry, but a few can (among them: Burton Watson, A.C. Graham, Arthur Waley, Jonathan Chaves). And there are the poets: most know no Chinese, a few know some. Kenneth Rexroth belonged to this last category (along with Gary Snyder and the later Pound)—although this particular example is perhaps more "imitation" than translation.

Rexroth ignores what he presumably dislikes, or feels cannot be translated, in the original. The title is eliminated, and the philosophical *empty mountain* becomes the empirical *mountain wilderness*. Certain words and phrases are his own invention. One of them, *where nobody ever comes* leads him into a trap: he must modify *the sound of a far off voice* with *something like*, and it makes a rather clutzy fourth line. But this is clearly the first *poem* of the group, able to stand by itself. It is the closest to the spirit, if not the letter, of the original: the poem Wang might have written had he been born a 20th century American.

Rexroth's great skill is apparent in three tiny gestures. In line 2, by using *comes* rather than the more obvious *goes* he has created an implicit narrator-observer (i.e., "comes here where I am") without using the first person. Second, he takes an utterly ordinary phrase, *once in a great while*, and lets us hear it, for the first time, as something lovely and onomatopoeic. And third, Rexroth's *slip* for Wang's *enter* is perhaps too sensual—reminiscent of Sanskrit forest trysts—but it is irresistible.

12

Deer Fence

Empty hills, no one in sight,

only the sound of someone talking;

late sunlight enters the deep wood,

shining over the green moss again.

—Burton Watson, 1971

Watson is a prolific and particularly fine translator of classical Chinese and Japanese poetry, history and philosophy; he is comparable only to Arthur Waley in this century. He was also the first scholar whose work displayed an affinity with the modernist revolution in American poetry: absolute precision, concision, and the use of everyday speech.

[Curiously, while most of the French and American modernists lit joss sticks at the altars of their newfound Chinese ancestors, the scholars of Chinese ignored, or were actively hostile to modern poetry. Many still are. Chinese poets were, however, excited by the doings in the West. Hu Shi's 1917 manifestoes, which launched the "Chinese Renaissance" in literature by rejecting classical language and themes in favor of vernacular and "realism", were largely inspired by Ezra Pound's 1913 Imagist manifestoes. Full circle: Pound thought he found it in China, Hu Shi thought it came from the West.]

Watson here renders the first two characters of line 1 with two words; no article, no explanation. His presentation of the image is as direct as the Chinese. There are 24 English words (six per line) for the Chinese 20, yet every word of the Chinese has been translated without indulging, as others have done, in a telegraphic minimalism. In the translation of Chinese poetry, as in everything, nothing is more difficult than simplicity.

More than arrangements of tones, rhymes, and number of characters per line, Chinese poetry, like all ancient poetries, is based on parallelism: the dual (*yin-yang*) nature of the universe. Wang's first two lines are typical: *see no people/ but hear people*. He even repeats a character. Watson retains Wang's parallelism effortlessly enough (*no one/someone*) yet he is the first translator to do so.

13

Deer Enclosure

Empty mountain: no man is seen,

But voices of men are heard.

Sun's reflection reaches into the woods

And shines upon the green moss.

—Wai-lim Yip, 1972

Yip is a critic who has written brilliantly on the importance of Chinese poetics to 20th century American poetry. As a translator he is less successful, perhaps because English is apparently his second language. (It is rarely possible, though many try, to translate *out* of one's natural language.) Thus the strangeness of *no man is seen* and the oddly anthropomorphic *reaches into*.

Like Burton Watson, Yip follows Wang's repetition of *person* in the first two lines (though his *persons* are *men*) and presents six English words per line for the Chinese five. But unlike Watson and the other translators, Yip actually gives us *less* than the original—leaving out *deep* and *again*.

In a later version of this translation, published in his anthology *Chinese Poetry* (University of California Press, 1976), Yip clipped the first line to the almost pidgin *Empty mountain: no man.*

14

Deer Park

Hills empty, no one to be seen

We hear only voices echoed—

With light coming back into the deep wood

The top of the green moss is lit again.

—G.W. Robinson, 1973

Robinson's translation, published by Penguin Books, is, unhappily, the most widely available edition of Wang in English.

In this poem Robinson not only creates a narrator, he makes it a group, as though it were a family outing. With that one word, *we*, he effectively scuttles the mood of the poem.

Reading the last word of the poem as *top*, he offers an image that makes little sense on the forest floor: one would have to be small indeed to think of moss vertically.

For a jolt to the system, try reading this aloud.

15

En la Ermita del Parque de los Venados

No se ve gente en este monte.

Sólo se oyen, lejos, voces.

Por los ramajes la luz rompe.

Tendida entre la yerba brilla verde.

—Octavio Paz, 1974

[*In the Deer Park Hermitage*. No people are seen on this mountain./ Only voices, far off, are heard./ Light breaks through the branches./ Spread among the grass it shines green.]

For the second (1978) edition of *Versiones y Diversiones*, his selected translations, Paz wrote:

The translation of this poem is particularly difficult, for the poem carries to an extreme the characteristics of Chinese poetry: universality, impersonality, absence of time, absence of subject. In Wang Wei's poem, the solitude of the mountain is so great that not even the poet himself is present. After a number of attempts I wrote these four unrhymed lines: three with nine syllables each and the last with eleven.

Months later, reading some Mahayana texts, I was surprised by the frequency with which the Western paradise, domain of the Amida Buddha, is mentioned. I remembered that Wang Wei had been a fervent Buddhist: I consulted one of his biographies and discovered that his devotion for Amida was such that he had written a hymn in which he speaks of his desire to be reborn in the Western Paradise—the place of the setting sun . . .

This is nature poetry, but a Buddhist nature poetry: does not the quatrain reflect, even more than the naturalistic aestheticism traditional in this kind of composition, a spiritual experience? Sometime later, Burton Watson, who knows my love for Chinese poetry, sent me his *Chinese Lyricism*. There I encountered a confirmation of my suspicion: for Wang Wei the light of the setting sun had a very precise meaning. An allusion to the Amida Buddha: at the end of the afternoon the adept meditates and, like the moss in the forest, receives illumination. Poetry perfectly objective, impersonal, far from the mysticism of a St. John of the Cross, but no less authentic or profound than that of the Spanish poet. Transformation of man and nature before the divine light, although in a sense inverse to that of Western tradition. In place of the humanization of the world that surrounds us, the Oriental spirit is impregnated with the objectivity, passivity and impersonality of the trees, grass and rocks, so that, impersonally, it receives the impartial light of a revelation that is also impersonal. Without losing the

reality of the trees, rocks and earth, Wang Wei's mountain and forest are emblems of the void. Imitating his reticence, I limited myself to lightly changing the last two lines:

> No se ve gente en este monte.
> Sólo se oyen, lejos, voces.
> La luz poniente rompe entre las ramas.
> En la yerba tendida brilla verde.

[No people are seen on this mountain./ Only voices, far off, are heard./ Western light breaks through the branches./ Spread over the grass it shines green.]

Paz drops *empty* from the first line; in the second, like Margouliès and Rexroth, he makes the voices *far off*. His third line, though not strictly literal, may be the most beautiful of all the versions: replacing the abstract *light enters the forest* with the concrete and dramatic *light breaks through the branches*—the light almost becoming the sudden illumination, *satori*, of Zen Buddhism. In the fourth line, the *moss* has become *grass*, no doubt because the Spanish word for moss, *musgo*, is unpleasantly squishy. (How mossy—soft and damp—is the English *moss*!)

What is missing from these lovely third and fourth lines is the cyclical quality of the original. Wang begins both lines with *to return*: taking a specific time of day and transforming it into a moment, frozen in its recurrence, that becomes cosmic. Reading the image as a metaphor for illumination, the ordinary (sunset in the forest) represents the extraordinary (the enlightenment of the individual) which, in terms of the cosmos, is as ordinary as sunlight illuminating a patch of moss.

An endless series of negations: The mountain seems *empty* (without people) because no one's in sight. But people are heard, so the mountain is not *empty*. But the mountain is *empty* because it is an illusion. The light from the Western Paradise, the light called *shadow* falls.

16
Li Ch'ai

In empty mountains no one can be seen.

But here might echoing voices cross.

Reflecting rays

        entering the deep wood

Glitter again

        on the dark green moss.

—William McNaughton, 1974

McNaughton offers the Chinese place-name as a title, but his transliteration is incorrect—something like *Beer Park*.

Line 1 has been turned into a general statement, almost a parody of Eastern Wisdom: in an empty glass there is no liquid. Line 2 places the action *here* for no reason and adds *cross* for the rhyme scheme he has imposed on himself. (Not much rhymes with *moss*; it's something of an albatross. But he might have attempted an Elizabethan pastoral *echoing voices toss* or perhaps a half-Augustan, half-Dada *echoing voices sauce*.)

Splitting the last couplet into four lines is apparently an attempt at pictorial representation. The last line adds *dark* to fill out the thumpety-thump.

17

Clos aux cerfs

Montagne déserte. Personne n'est en vue.

Seuls, les échos des voix résonnent, au loin.

Ombres retournent dans la forêt profonde:

Dernier éclat de la mousse, vert.

—François Cheng, 1977

[*Deer Enclosure*. Deserted mountain. No one in sight./ Only, the echoes of voices resound, far off./ Shadows return to the deep forest:/ Last gleaming of the moss, green.]

Cheng writes:

[Wang] describes here a walk on the mountain, which is at the same time a spiritual experience, an experience of the Void and of communion with Nature. The first couplet should be interpreted "On the empty mountain I meet no one; only some echoes of voices of people walking come to me." But through the suppression of the personal pronoun and of locative elements the poet identifies himself immediately with the "empty mountain," which is therefore no longer merely a "complement of place"; similarly, in the third line he *is* the ray of the setting sun that penetrates the forest. From the point of view of content, the first two lines present the poet as still "not seeing"; in his ears the echoes of human voices still resound. The last two lines are centered in the theme of "vision": to see the golden effect of the setting sun on the green moss. Seeing here signifies illumination and deep communion with the essence of things. Elsewhere the poet often omits the personal pronoun to effect the description of *actions in sequence* where human acts are related to movements in nature.

(tr. Donald Riggs & Jerome Seaton)

Cheng also presents a literal translation of the poem:

> Montagne vide / ne percevoir personne
> Seulement entendre / voix humaine résonner
> Ombre-retournée / penetrer forêt profonde
> Encore luire / sur la mousse verte

It is curious to see how Cheng poeticizes and even Westernizes his literal version to create a finished translation. The Buddhist *montagne vide* (empty mountain) becomes the Romantic *montagne déserte* (deserted mountain). *Échos* and *au loin* (far off) are added to the second line. In the third, his literal *ombre-retournée* (returned shadow—a trope he notes as mean-

ing "rays of sunset") has become a subject and verb, *ombres retournent* (shadows return) which considerably alters the meaning. Cheng's last line is quite peculiar: the literal *Encore luire sur la mousse verte* (to shine again on the green moss) becomes *Dernier éclat de la mousse, vert* (last gleaming of the moss, green—the green referring to the gleaming, not the moss). The line owes more to French Symbolists than to Tang Buddhists.

Translations aside, Cheng's book is a luminous, original study of Chinese poetry. In the English version, published in 1982, Jerome P. Seaton, working "after the interpretations of" Cheng, offers a translation that seems to owe more to Gary Snyder's 1978 poem (#19) than to Cheng:

DEER PARK

Empty mountain. None to be seen.
But hear, the echoing of voices.
Returning shadows enter deep, the grove.
Sun shines, again, on lichen's green.

18

The Deer Park

Not the shadow on a man on the deserted hill—

And yet one hears voices speaking;

Deep in the seclusion of the woods,

Stray shafts of the sun pick out the green moss.

—H.C. Chang, 1977

Chang translates 12 of Wang's 20 words, and makes up the rest.

In line 1 the first *on* is probably a typographical error, but in such surroundings, it's hard to tell. In any event, what's that *shadow* doing (or more exactly, not doing) there? Only the shadow knows.

Why are the *shafts* of sun *stray*? Why are they *shafts* at all? And why do they *pick out* the moss? The verb is unavoidably reminiscent of the consumption of winkles and crab.

In short, the poem is more Chang than Wang. (It is taken from a three-volume set, all by the same translator, and published, oddly, by Columbia University Press.)

19

Empty mountains:

   no one to be seen.

Yet—hear—

   human sounds and echoes.

Returning sunlight

   enters the dark woods;

Again shining

   on the green moss, above.

—Gary Snyder, 1978

Surely one of the best translations, partially because of Snyder's lifelong forest experience. Like Rexroth, he can *see* the scene. Every word of Wang has been translated, and nothing added, yet the translation exists as an American poem.

Changing the passive *is heard* to the imperative *hear* is particularly beautiful, and not incorrect: it creates an exact moment, which is now. Giving us both meanings, *sounds and echoes*, for the last word of line 2 is, like most sensible ideas, revolutionary. Translators always assume that only one reading of a foreign word or phrase may be presented, despite the fact that perfect correspondence is rare.

The poem ends strangely. Snyder takes the last word, which everyone else has read as *on*, and translates it with its alternative meaning, *above*, isolating it from the phrase with a comma. What's going on? Moss presumably is only above if one is a rock or bug. Or are we meant to look up, after seeing the moss, back toward the sun: the vertical metaphor of enlightenment?

In answer to my query, Snyder wrote: "The reason for '. . . moss, above' . . . is that the sun is entering (in its sunset sloping, hence 'again'—a final shaft) the woods, and illuminating some moss *up in the trees.* (NOT ON ROCKS.) This is how my teacher Ch'en Shih-hsiang saw it, and my wife (Japanese) too, the first time she looked at the poem."

The point is that translation is more than a leap from dictionary to dictionary; it is a reimagining of the poem. As such, every reading of every poem, regardless of language, is an act of translation: translation into the reader's intellectual and emotional life. As no individual reader remains the same, each reading becomes a different—not merely another—reading. The same poem cannot be read twice.

Snyder's explanation is only one moment, the latest, when the poem suddenly transforms before our eyes. Wang's 20 characters remain the same, but the poem continues in a state of restless change.

Further Comments

Eliot Weinberger's commentary on the successive translations of Wang Wei's little poem illustrates, with succinct clarity, not only the evolution of the art of translation in the modern period but at the same time the changes in poetic sensibility. His examples come from English and, to a lesser extent, from French; I am sure that a parallel exploration of German or Italian would produce similar results. Weinberger cites only one Spanish version, my own. There may be another, and perhaps one or two in Portuguese. One must admit, however, that Spanish and Portuguese do not enjoy a *corpus* of Chinese translation similar in importance or quality to that of other languages. This is regrettable: the modern era has discovered other classicisms besides that of Greco–Roman culture, and one of them is China and Japan.

Weinberger's commentary led me back to my own translation. Probably the greatest difficulty for any translator of a Chinese poem is the unique temper of the language and of the writing. The majority of the poems in the *Shi jing*, the most ancient collection of Chinese poetry, are written in lines of four syllables that are four characters/words. For example, the phonetic transcription of the first line of a small erotic poem in the *Shi jing* is composed of these four monosyllables: *Xing nu qi shu*. The literal translation is: *Sweet girl how pretty*. It is not impossible to transform this phrase into a line from a ballad: *¡Qué linda la dulce niña!* or *How lovely the pretty maiden!* Five words and eight syllables, twice the original. Arthur Waley thought to resolve the prosodic problem by having each Chinese monosyllable correspond to a tonic accent in the English line. The result was English lines that were quite long, but with the same number of accents as the Chinese original. This method, besides being not terribly perfect, is inapplicable to Spanish: in our language words generally have more syllables than English iambic pentameter. Our line has either three accents (in the fourth syllable, in the seventh or eighth, and in the tenth) or only two (in the sixth and the tenth). In contrast, the English line has five accents or rhythmic beats. Furthermore, in English the number of syllables may vary; not only do we have more consonants, but we may also rely on a rich assonance. The great advantage of the assonant is that the rhyme becomes a distant echo, one which never exactly repeats the endings of the previous line. I will note, finally, a small similarity between Chinese and Spanish versification: in Chinese poetry only paired verses are rhymed, exactly like our *romances* and traditional assonant poems.

The first to attempt to make English poems out of Chinese originals was Ezra Pound. All of us since who have translated Chinese and Japanese poetry are not only his followers but his debtors. I never found Pound's theory of translating Chinese persuasive, and in other writings I have tried to explain my reasons. It doesn't matter: though his theories seemed unreliable, his practice not only convinced me but, literally, enchanted me. Pound did not attempt to find metrical equivalents or rhymes: taking off from the images-ideograms of the originals, he wrote English poems in free verse. Those poems had (and still have) an enormous poetic freshness; at the same time they allow us to glimpse another civilization, and one quite distant from Western Greco–Roman tradition.

The poems of *Cathay* (1915) were written in an energetic language and in irregular verses which I have rather loosely labeled as free. In fact, although they do not have fixed measures, each one of them is a verbal unity. Nothing could be more remote from the prose chopped into short lines that today passes for free verse. Do Pound's poems correspond to the originals? A useless question: Pound *invented*, as Eliot said, Chinese poetry in English. The points of departure were some ancient Chinese poems, revived and changed by a great poet; the result was other poems. Others: the same. With that small volume of translations Pound, to a great extent, began modern poetry in English. Yet, at the same time, he also began something unique: the modern tradition of classical Chinese poetry in the poetic conscience of the West.

Pound's effort was a success, and after *Cathay* many

others followed on various paths. I am thinking above all of Arthur Waley. The translations of Chinese and Japanese poetry into English have been so great and so diverse that they themselves form a chapter in the modern poetry of the language. I find nothing similar in French, although there are notable translations, such as those by Claude Roy or François Cheng. Certainly we owe to Claudel, Segalen, and Saint–John Perse poetic visions of China—but not memorable translations. It's a pity. In Spanish this lack has impoverished us.

In my own isolated attempts I followed, at first, the examples of Pound and, more than anyone, Waley—a ductile talent, but one less intense and less powerful. Later, little by little, I found my own way. At the beginning I used free verse; later I tried to adjust myself to a fixed rule, without of course attempting to reproduce Chinese meter. In general, I have endeavored to retain the number of lines of each poem, not to scorn assonances and to respect, as much as possible, the parallelism. This last element is central to Chinese poetry, but neither Pound nor Waley gave it the attention it deserves. Nor do the other translators in English. It is a serious omission not only because parallelism is the nucleus of the best Chinese poets and philosophers: the *yin* and the *yang*. The unity that splits into dualty to reunite and to divide again. I would add that parallelism links, however slightly, our own indigenous Mexican poetry with that of China.

In the Han era they moved from a four–syllable line to one of five and seven (*gu shi*). These poems are composed in a strict tonal counterpoint. (The classical language has four tones.) The number of lines is undefined and only paired lines are rhymed. During the Tang period versification became more strict and they wrote poems of eight and four lines (*lu shi* and *jue qu*, respectively). The lines of those poems are, as in the earlier style, composed of five and seven syllables; the same rhyme is used throughout the poem. The other rules apply to parallelism (the four lines in the center of the poem must form two antithetical couplets) and the tonal structure. This last recalls, in certain respects, classical quantitative versification—although the rhythm does not come from the combination of short and long syllables but rather from the alternation of tones. Every Chinese poem offers a true counterpoint that cannot be reproduced in any Indo–European language. I will spare the reader the chart of the various combinations (two for the five syllable lines and two for the seven). There are other forms: the *ci* (*tz'u*), poetry written to accompany already existing musical tunes and with lines of unequal length; dramatic verse (*qu*) and the lyric-dramatic (*san qu*).

Wang Wei's poem is written in four lines of five syllables each (*jue qu*); the second line rhymes with the fourth. In order to transmit the information of the original, while attempting to recreate the poem in Spanish, I decided to use a line of nine syllables. I chose this meter not only because of its greater amplitude but also because it appeared to be, without actually being, a truncated hendecasyllable. It is the least traditional of our meters and it appears infrequently in Spanish poetry, except among the "modernists"—above all, Ruben Darío—who used it a great deal. I also decided to use assonant rhyme, but unlike the Chinese original I rhymed all four lines. The poem is divided into two parts. The first alludes to the solitude of the forest, and aural rather than visual sensations predominate (no one is seen, only voices are heard). The second refers to the apparition of light in a forest clearing and is composed of silently visual sensations: the light breaks through the branches, falls on the moss and, in a manner of speaking, rises again. Attentive to this sensual and spiritual division, I divided the poem into two pairs: the first line rhymes with the second and the third rhymes with the fourth. I left the two first lines of my earlier version intact, but I radically changed the third and the fourth lines:

No se ve gente en este monte,
sólo se oyen, lejos, voces.
Bosque profundo. Luz poniente:
alumbra el musgo y, verde, asciende.

[No people are seen on this mountain,/ only voices, far-off,
are heard./ Deep forest. Western light:/ it illuminates the moss
and, green, rises.]

The first two lines need no explanation. It seems to me that
I succeeded in transmitting the information while conserving
the impersonality of the original: the I is implicit. The third
line, according to François Cheng, means literally: *returning
shadow—to penetrate—deep—forest*. Cheng points out that *re-
turning shadow* alludes to the western sun. James J.Y. Liu trans-
lates in similar terms but, with greater propriety, says *reflected
light* in place of *returning shadow*. In his literary version Liu
writes: *The reflected sunlight pierces the deep forest*. Cheng has
Ombres retournent dans la forêt profonde. The reader, through a
note at the foot of the page, learns that *ombres retournent*—a
rather forced trope—means the rays of the setting sun. And
why shadows and not light or brightness or something similar?
I wavered a great deal about translating this line. First I wrote:
Cruza el follaje el sol poniente. (The western sun crosses the
foliage.) But the poet does not speak of foliage but rather of
the forest. I then tried: *Traspasa el bosque el sol poniente*. (The
western sun crosses through the forest.) Somewhat better, but
perhaps too energetic, too active. Next I decided to omit the
verb, as Spanish allowed the ellipsis. The two syntactical blocks
(*bosque profundo/luz poniente*; deep forest/western light) pre-
served the impersonality of the original and at the same time
alluded to the silent ray of light crossing through the over-
growth.

According to Cheng the last line means: *still—to shine—
on—green—moss*. Liu says: *again—shine—green—moss—upon*.
That is: the reflection is green. In his literal version Weinberger

includes all of the possibilities: *to return/again—to shine/to re-flect—green/blue/black—moss/lichen—above/on(top of)/top*. In two places my version departs from the others. First: the western light *illuminates* the moss—in place of reflecting it or shining on it—because the verb *illuminate* contains both the physical aspect of the phenomenon (shining, light, clarity, brightness) and the spiritual (to illuminate understanding). Second: I say that the green reflection *ascends* or *rises* because I want to accentuate the spiritual character of the scene. The light of the western sun refers to the point of the horizon ruled by the Amida Buddha. Without trying to pin down the floating game of analogies, one might say that the western sun is the spiritual light of the paradise of the West, the cardinal point of the Amida Buddha; the solitude of the mountain and the forest is this world in which there is nobody really, though we hear the echoes of voices; and the clearing in the forest illuminated by the silent ray of light is the one who meditates and contemplates.

—Octavio Paz

Postscript

After the publication of these commentaries in the Mexican magazine *Vuelta*, the editors received a furious letter from a professor at the Colegio de México, charging me with nothing less than "crimes against Chinese poetry." Among those criminal acts was the "curious neglect" of "Boodberg's cedule."

The cryptic reference, I later discovered, was to *Cedules from a Berkeley Workshop in Asiatic Philology*, a series of essays privately published by Prof. Peter A. Boodberg in 1954 and 1955. The relevant essay, "Philology in Translation–Land," is 1½ pages long and is devoted to excoriating, in idiosyncratic language, all other translators and scholars of Wang Wei for failing to realize that the last word of the poem, *shang* (which now means *above, on [top of], top*) had an alternate meaning in the Tang dynasty: *to rise*.

This usage apparently dropped out of the language centuries ago. But for those who doubt the accuracy of poetry translated by poets rather than scholars, it should be noted that Octavio Paz, in his latest version of the poem, intuitively divined this forgotten meaning and translated the word as *asciende*.

Boodberg ends his "cedule" with his own version of the poem, which he calls "a still inadequate, yet philologically correct, rendition of the stanza (with due attention to grapho–syntactic overtones and enjambment)":

The empty mountain: to see no men,
Barely earminded of men talking—countertones,
And antistrophic lights–and–shadows incoming deeper the
    deep–treed grove
Once more to glowlight the blue–green mosses—going up
    (The empty mountain . . .)

To me this sounds like Gerard Manley Hopkins on LSD, and I am grateful to the furious professor for sending me in search of this, the strangest of the many Weis.

—E.W.

Sources

Bynner, Witter & Kiang Kang-hu. *The Jade Mountain*. New York: Alfred A. Knopf, 1929.

Chang, H.C. *Chinese Literature, Vol II: Nature Poetry*. New York: Columbia University Press, 1977.

Chen, C.J. & Michael Bullock. *Poems of Solitude*. Rutland, Vt. & Tokyo: Charles E. Tuttle, 1960.

Cheng, François. *L'écriture poetique chinoise*. Paris: Editions du Seuil, 1977. [English translation: *Chinese Poetic Writing*. trans. by Donald A. Riggs & Jerome P. Seaton. Bloomington: Indiana University Press, 1982.]

Fletcher, W.J.B. *Gems of Chinese Verse*. Shanghai: n.pb.l., 1919.

Jenyns, Soame. *Further Poems of the T'ang Dynasty*. London: John Murray, 1944.

Liu, James J.Y. *The Art of Chinese Poetry*. Chicago: University of Chicago Press, 1962.

McNaughton, William. *Chinese Literature*. Rutland, Vt.: Charles E. Tuttle, 1974.

Margouliès, G. *Anthologie Raisonée de la Littérature Chinoise*. Paris: Payot, 1948.

Paz, Octavio. *Versiones y Diversiones*. Mexico City: Joaquín Mortiz, 1974 (revised edition, 1978).

Rexroth, Kenneth. *Love and the Turning Year*. New York: New Directions, 1970.

Robinson, G.W. *Poems of Wang Wei*. Harmondsworth, U.K.: Penguin Books, 1973.

Snyder, Gary. *Journal for the Protection of All Beings*. No. 4, Fall 1978.

Wang Wei. *Hiding the Universe*. trans. by Wai-lim Yip. New York: Munshinsha/Grossman, 1972.

Wang Wei. *Poems*. trans. by Chang Yin-nan & Lewis Walmsley. Rutland, Vt. & Tokyo: Charles E. Tuttle, 1958.

Watson, Burton. *Chinese Lyricism*. New York: Columbia University Press, 1971.